The Woman and the Whale

Previous Books by Ethel Mortenson Davis

A Gatherer, of days and lights and secret places. 2021. Sturgeon Bay, WI: Four Windows Press.

A Letter of the Horizon's Poem. 2019. American Forks, UT: Kelsay Books, Inc.

Under the Tail of the Milky Way Galaxy. 2018. Sturgeon Bay, WI: Four Windows Press.

Here We Breathe In Sky and Out Sky, Poems of New Mexico. 2016. Sturgeon Bay, WI: Four Windows Press.

The Healer (chapbook). 2016. Sturgeon Bay, WI: Four Windows Press.

White Ermine Across her Shoulders. 2011. Bloomington. IN: iUniverse, Inc.

I Sleep Between the Moons of New Mexico. 2010. New York, NY: iUniverse, Inc.

The Woman and the Whale

Encounters with Other Kingdoms

Poems

By Ethel Mortenson Davis

Four Windows Press

Four Windows Press
Sturgeon Bay, WI 54235

Fourwindowspress1@gmail.com

Copyright © 2024 by Ethel Mortenson Davis

All rights reserved. No part of this publication may be reproduced, distributed or transmitted in any form or by any means, without prior written permission.

Ethel Mortenson Davis
231 N Hudson Ave.
Sturgeon Bay, Wisconsin 54235
davisethel@gmail.com

Publisher's Note: This is a work of poetry. Names, characters, places, and incidents are a product of the author's imagination. Locales and public names are sometimes used for atmospheric purposes. Any resemblance to actual people, living or dead, or to businesses, companies, events, institutions, or locales is completely coincidental.

Book Layout © 2017 BookDesignTemplates.com
Cover Art and Design by Ethel Mortenson Davis

The Woman and the Whale -- 1st ed.
ISBN 979-8-9905946-1-6

Dedication

To all those people whose faces become recognizable to animals and birds as helpers and saviors.

Acknowledgments

I am grateful to the editors of the following publications in which my poems previously appeared:

"Ancestors," *Moss Piglet*, John Bloner, Jr. Ed., October 2022, p. 18.
"Elephant Track," *Moss Piglet*, January 2020, John Bloner, Jr., Ed., p. 14.
"Master," *Poetry Hall, Chinese and English Bilingual Journal*, Issue 25. Published in both English and as translated into Chinese.
"Missing," *Poetry Hall, Chinese and English Bilingual Journal*, Issue 16, Vol. 5, No. 2, August 10, 2022, p. 116. Published in both English and as translated into Chinese.
"Suspension," *Poetry Hall, Chinese and English Bilingual Journal*, Issue 16, Vol. 5, No. 2, August 10, 2022, p. 117. Published in both English and as translated into Chinese.
"The Elk," *Moss Piglet*, January 2023, John Bloner, Jr., Ed., pg. 79.
"The Hunter," *Poetry Hall, Chinese and English Bilingual Journal*, Issue 25. Published in both English and as translated into Chinese.
"The Deer," *I Sleep Between the Moons of New Mexico*. Sturgeon Bay, Wisconsin, Four Windows Press, 2010, p. 75.
"The Woman and the Whale," *Moss Piglet*, John Bloner, Jr. Ed., October 2024.
"Why Night Was Made," *Poetry Breakfast*, August 8, 2023. Accessed at https://poetrybreakfast.com/2023/08/08/why-night-was-made-a-poem-by-ethel-mortenson.

I am grateful to our poetry group, Unabridged, who are dedicated to help us write beautiful and meaningful poetry.

CONTENTS

The Woman and the Whale 11
Whale Song 12
The Wind and The Bird 13
Why Night Was Made 14
The Deer 15
You Must Tell Me 16
The Elk 17
Tipping Point 18
Wholly Human 19
Smallness 20
Patches 21
Petals 22
Answers 23
Laughing As He Went 24
Lost Memories 25
Mask Of Sorrow 26
Master 27
Monarch's Wings 28
Moon 29
Hummingbird 30
Home 31
Elephant Track 32
Hope 33
Bird 34
Vision 35
We Grew Close to That Land 36

Song of the Holy Woman 37
Suspension 38
Story of the Marriage of Two Souls 39
The Hunter 40
Belongings 41
Ancestors 42
Summer's Light 44
Orchid Room 45
Secret Garden 46
Who Would I See? 47
Anytime 48
Butterfly 49
Chimney Swifts 50
Differences 51
Conversation 52
Fawn 53
Forever 54
The Goddess 55
Hard To Believe 56
Honoring 57
Howling 58
Letter From the Earth 59
Life 60
Maple Sugar Moon 61
Missing 62
Never Again 63
Path 64
Red Pine Bark 65
Retirement Party 66
Snowbound 67
The Speed of Light 68

Where My Heart Lies 69
You Would Be happy, Francha 70
Present 71
There is Still Time 72
ABOUT THE AUTHOR 73

The Woman and the Whale

The day was a day of celebration.
A small whale stood vertical,
head out of the water,
straight up in the air,
his dorsal fins reaching like arms
toward the sky.

A woman marine biologist
from a South Pacific Island
said the whale tried to tuck her
under his dorsal fin
when she interacted with him.

At first, she struggled to get away—
until she saw the tiger shark
circling her, trying to get at her.
The whale kept his body between
the diver and the shark.

Then the whale grew agitated,
slapped his tail at the shark
before finally running it off.

Today, the whale came back with his family,
many heads sticking straight up in the air.

Whale Song

There are people in the South Seas
that say they are descended from whales,
that their ancestors were from the family of Artiodactyla.

A Māori woman is working to bring personhood
to the whales, to say that whales are people
and have the right to life as we do.

If she succeeds, we will be thankful
she has saved some of the whales—
some of her people.

The Wind and The Bird

The down comforter hung on the clothesline.
Wind stirred it and awakened its feathers
(for it had been asleep for many years)
and lit its wings on fire.

He rose up, wanting to fly,
wanting to be a bird,
remembering what stars
looked like in the night sky,

remembering wind currents
that carried him up on billowing sheets of air,
remembering how happy he was
to be with his old friend the wind,
to be a bird, again.

Why Night Was Made

I'm sure night was made
when man invented war
so that darkness would
put her arms around him,
slowing him down
so that he could think things over
and then at dawn
start new again.

I'm sure night was made
when war came to this family,
breath knocked out of the man,
the woman and child
languishing in the street.
Darkness would give them
a few moments of relief.

I'm sure darkness was made
when man invented war.

The Deer

You came to the edge of the woods today
to catch my eye.
My dog did not see you, though,
young girl-deer.

You came to tell me, "Thank you,"
or so it seemed that way,
for digging you out of the mud yesterday.

Flailing, you were caught up to your neck.
My dog and I saw you
throwing your head from side to side, exhausted—
on our walk in the rain-soaked morning.

Two came to dig you out,
and, after resting, you got up
and ran away.

So today you came back with gratitude,
or your face looked that way—
like my long-lost daughter.
You came to make me understand
that you were full of thankfulness,
to catch my eye,
or so it seemed that way.

You Must Tell Me

The earth
did not tell me
before she locked
the land in drought,
shriveling the crops
into nothingness.

The cardinal did not know
wildfires were raging
until he flew through them,
his feathers burned
off his head and chest.
He barely looked
like a cardinal.

But you,
you must tell me
before you leave me.

The Elk

The old man
loves the warmth of the sun
even though he is immobile,
loves to breathe
the scent of autumn
even at the end of his days.
Here, at this entrance to the pasture,
we panic within ourselves,
knowing time is running low,
and we have nothing left
in our quiver for tomorrow
when the elk returns and stands
to give himself to us.

Tipping Point

Are we at a tipping point
in our world?
Falling back down
a steep precipice
where ecosystems
can no longer be restored?
No longer healed?

Like the wolf
struggling in the trap
this night,
and you saying
he is nothing more
than refuse
on top of the earth.

He, who is part
of an intricate system
more beautiful than you
can imagine.

Are we at a tipping point,
you and me,
falling off the brow of a cliff?
Can we ever begin
to have a conversation?

Wholly Human

Fannie Lou Hamer
was beaten by a policeman
until he couldn't beat her any longer,
so, he had his partner continue
the beating.

That day, Fannie Lou
left part of her brain
there on the ground,
but she didn't leave her courage.
She came back for more.

Because she only wanted
her people to be free,
free from fear,
free from beatings,
free from death—
just free to enjoy life,
to be wholly human.

Smallness

We set our own perimeters,
our own truth.
We put out our stakes
and say this is our life's philosophy.

The elephant's philosophy
is her waterhole:
one waterhole to the next,
one food source to another.

But the bird's philosophy
is vast—across continents.

But we love setting out fences,
enjoying windowsills and back yards,
giving into our smallness.

Patches

To Lorraine Wells

Patches
was a three-colored cat,
the best mouser we ever had,
a smart, independent, female feline,

until the day
we brought home King,
our new dog.

Patches did not like him.
He hated her,
so, she left home.
The neighbors said
she moved in with them—
became their cat.

After a year and a half,
Patches came back home,
cuddled up to King.

He loved her. They slept together.
The smartest cat we ever had.

Petals

Climbing into the mountains, the wilderness
unfolds her petals one at a time,
exposing her mysterious splendor.

And in the center of our frailty,
loneliness flees our human heart,
and we are filled with each new discovery—

like the young male deer
who catches the corner of my eye,
standing perfectly still,
hoping I will not notice him.

Answers

I have come to the forest again,
seeking an answer to a question.

Emaciated fox turns to let me know
he is aware of my presence.
The new wren whispers,
"Go too far until you lose yourself
and know nothing of time and space.
Then you will find the answers
to all your questions."

Each day I go a bit further into the forest
and find an unexpected answer.

Laughing As He Went

Now they want to clip
the ears of the Gray Wolf,
clip the wolves back
until they're almost decimated,
weakening their packs
to almost extinction.

The native tribes of Wisconsin and Montana
 have stood up for the wolf.
They see themselves parallel to the wolf.
They too were killed back
to almost extinction,
starved and hounded,
brothers to the wolf
in life and suffering.

The hunters carry away
the great, large bodies of wolves
in their arms,
laughing as they go.

I remember the Gray Wolf
that morning as he rolled
down a steep embankment,
looking like a great ball
of white and gray fur,
laughing as he went.

Lost Memories

To Kevin Michael Davis

The memories of you are still real,
who you were and what you did.

But now that you are gone,
and everyone who knew you will someday be gone,
what will happen to your memories?

Are they lost forever?
Or will they be written down in a remembrance book,
kept there in a wild garden along this Great Lake?

Will the red cedars form the book's binding?
The wild snow geese the white pages?

Will your memories mingle with other people's,
strolling together in a blue-perfumed night?

Mask Of Sorrow

I will wear
the Mask of Sorrow
for all the lost birds
in our world.

I will wear
the Mask of Sadness
for all the animals and plants
that have disappeared.

I will wear
The Mask of Grief
for you,
even though it was forced upon me,
and I did not want it.

But I will wear the mask anyhow,
until my face
grows into it and over it.

Master

To Mary Wood, Sonja Bingen, and Estella Lauter

The teacher awakened the sleeping children
lost in a wintery, deep unconsciousness
and stirred them to stand up on wobbly legs.

Soon, they raised themselves up and started to run
toward the warming sun like newborn colts
that stand up shaking and, by days end,
are running free over field and stream,
anxiously looking for the next horizon.

Monarch's Wings

The Monarch butterfly
reminds me of long, sunset beaches
or the insides of lush, sweet melons,
wings moving in twitching, patting sounds
along tall milkweed towers
(some as tall as your head)
bringing sucking sounds
to lavender flowers
that smell like honey tastes—

never noticing
the round, soft bumblebee
upturned
at the end of the path,
legs pointed up to the sky.

Moon

The moon is most beautiful
at her beginning, or end.
Like a fine-edged sickle
punctuating the blackness.

Minimal.
A lot like you.
Not outstanding.
Almost missed.
Nevertheless beautiful.

Step outside with me.
We'll see her
from the steps.
Let your skin
touch the cold.

Hummingbird

A surprise.
Little one came
to the tip of the fern,
near my cheek,
cherishing the rain drops
falling from my fountain spring.
Stopped
and then stretched
his wings,
leaving momentarily
only to return
for one last relish.

Two beings connecting
in a momentary embrace.

Home

A Norwegian walked
across Antarctica.
He said to embrace
the silent, white landscape
and black, starry night.

Your cells come out of you,
he said, and become one
with the wilderness.

Like the caged bird
that wants to go home,
we need to return to our wilderness,
our home.

We've been gone a long time.

Elephant Track

Last night two men
slept close to an elephant trail,
hoping to see the herd.
In the morning,
they discovered an elephant track
between their two sleeping bags.

We are the same.
We are part of them,
they, part of us.

This morning, we ran
to catch a glimpse
of the last of October's light
as she lit the tops of trees on fire
and heard the voices of cranes,
high above our heads,
that we have heard
a thousand times before.

But still, we were lifted.

A great river
drifts through us.
She glimpses us
to see if we have caught
the ripples she throws out.

Hope

To Sophia and Erik Saucedo

Dear Grandmother,

Today your great, great granddaughter
is getting married
to a fine, young man,
and they promise their love
is greater than their parents' love
and their grandparents' love.
They promise they will be happier
than their parents were
or their grandparents.
And they promise their children
will be loved more than all
the ancestors put together.

Dear Grandmother,

This is their promise.
This is our hope.

Bird

You were what was needed
this morning
while the world was weeping,
flying along the path,
waiting for me to catchup,
playing your game
all the way
to the edge of the Great Lake.

You were what was needed
this morning while the world was weeping.

Vision

There is a painting
ready to be born,
pushing against the womb,
saying it is time—
now is the time—
to become, to be
a spirit of wonderment,
a pathway through
cherished clutter,
finally, to be let loose
in our world,
to lift us
        off our feet.

We Grew Close to That Land

To Deborah Anderson Hackl

We grew close
to that land
by walking the herds
to the night pastures.
Then, in the morning,
bringing them back
through the early light.

We grew close
to that land
by getting lost
in the overflowing banks
of the little creek
where the sounds
of peeping frogs
seemed to be everywhere,
even in the ditches
that lined the township roads.

We grew close
to that land,
but then we grew apart,
and now have rediscovered
a commonality between us
in the twilight of our lives.

Song of the Holy Woman

I awoke to the song
of a holy woman
beneath my window.

How beautiful her song,
I thought, but what is
she saying?

I rose to catch a glimpse
of her,
but I could not see her.

I ran to the other windows,
still hearing the song,
but she was not there.

Her song faded,
and I awoke
from the dream,

the dog on the floor
not stirring,
the song gone,
leaving an awakening.

Suspension

The suspended place in sleep
is where we yearn to be,
where we drift into eddies and flows,
being in the world
but not being there at all,

a place where flocks of birds
that fly in high altitudes
fall asleep but continue to fly forward,
suspended in the world
but not being there at all.

They count on some in the flock
to be awake and protect them from danger,
working in a community of dependence
held tightly by a greater wing.

Story of the Marriage of Two Souls

To Sophia and Erik Saucedo

The orchid dancer
worried all night
that the storm
would keep the two souls
from being married.

But the jumping waters
that dance into the sky
did not come.
The love of the village
was so great that it
pushed back the whirling winds.

The two souls were
finally married,
and everyone celebrated
long through the night.

An eagle had flown over
earlier that day
and told us it would be so.

The Hunter

To George Mortenson

I look for places
where deer could hide
in dense thickets
or in wetlands with tall reeds—
too hard for hunters to enter.

I remember you telling me
that you would see deer
lying down in the swamps,
water up to their faces,
hiding from approaching hunters.

You, who went out each day
during hunting season
to hunt deer,
then came back at night
to tell us
you saw nothing that day—

walking your land
but never raising the gun
to your chest.

Belongings

To Kevin Michael Davis

Your belongings arrived today,
clothing folded neatly and smelling clean,
books stacked along with your wallet and shaver.

At first, we didn't know what to think of it.
Thirteen years have passed away.
There was no letter of explanation, just two boxes.

So, we became like children and accepted the gift.

We became child-like and trusted those
that sent this treasure,
believing their meaning not meant to be harmful.

We, just glad to have something of you.

Ancestors

All my ancestors
live inside of me.

One Grandfather cut down
the biggest tree in the county.

My Mother said,
"Why didn't he leave
 the biggest tree
 to grow even bigger?"

Another Grandfather
referred to his trees
as "He and She."

"Save those orange seeds.
They will grow into trees."

One Grandmother said,
"What will they serve
for the wedding feast?
Rabbit?"

My room is filled
to the rafters
with their voices.

Every once in awhile
some ancestor
will sneak up behind me
and rudely nudge me
in the back

when I'm least
expecting it.

Summer's Light

Written after a painting by Margeret Lockwood entitled "Edge of Evening"

The light through the forest of trees
is the long-evening's glow
that lingers wistfully
on the sleeve of summer.

Here we stand and savor
each bite of brightness, each morsel,
rolling it over and over again
on our tongue

before winter's long reach of darkness
overtakes us and tells us
to keep in our place.

Orchid Room

For years
the orchids would not blossom—
until she placed them
on a sunny window
in the art gallery
filled with poetry books galore.

Soon,
the plants began to blossom
and thrive,
inspired by the poetry and art—
a place where they were allowed
to finally dream.

Secret Garden

Perfumed lotus blossom
hidden in the secret pond,
dark-water lover,
catches sight of cedar waxwing
in the berry-laden tree,
wishes she could fly.

Who Would I See?

Who would I see, baby wren,
if it wasn't for you?
Who would I see today, small robin,
so unsure of yourself,
if it wasn't for you?

If it wasn't for the new wildflowers
on my path this morning,
who would I see?
If it wasn't for the wet touch
of my old dog,
who would kiss me?

Anytime

Sometimes I want to go to you
but remember I have
put you in a special room
far from here,
a room, nonetheless,
with an open door,
so that I can enter
anytime.

So, I can see
your smile when you
were running with Shiva,
the golden lab,
through autumn leaves
in a special forest
long ago.
So, I can walk through that door
anytime.

Butterfly

I will leave the violet thistle
for your curled, thirsty tongue,
butterfly,
for the drought
has locked our land.

Chimney Swifts

There was always
a late spring night
when temperatures fell back down
so that my mother would build
one last fire in the wood stove.

In the morning, when she
went to open the stove's door,
nests from the chimney swifts
would be in the morning ash,
along with burnt-up baby birds.

Differences

Some,
who have traveled
through inhuman times,
disintegrate or fall
into a hardened core.
Others become whole
and choose to look for hope, escape.
They keep their wits about them
and gain power beyond belief.

Conversation

Tonight
the soft winds
will kiss me,
caressing every part of me.

Once you kissed me,
but now you have left me.
Once you cared for my islands,
my waters, my soils.
But now you have turned your back
on me.

The air between us
is not the same.
The days, the seasons
are no longer the same.

My heart is empty and yearning,
and I am alone.
Tonight, the wind will kiss me.

Fawn

Your spotted back fits well
in the dappled light of the wood—

as you wait utterly still
for the night and her returning.

Forever

Forever is not a word
in our universe.
Nothing in it
stays the same.
One day our earth
will become pieces
in the cosmic pond.

We are not forever.
Your movement
in the early morning
through the quiet rooms
will one day drift away.

Forever is not a word
in our universe.
One day we too
will have to part.

The Goddess

Kill her!
For her womanliness
is spilling out over her cloak,
strands of hair
falling across her face.

Soon, the whole world
will fall prostrate at her feet
and worship her again.
Then, we will lose our gods.

Beat her back.
We must hold our place
in this world.

Hard To Believe

Hard to believe
you were here once
and then evaporated
like the rain this morning
evaporating in the sun.

Hard to believe
you were here once,
warm and uneasy
with the world,
loving the southwest.
You said that place
never leaves you.

Then in that room, dying,
you apologized to your parents
for being gay.

We said, it doesn't matter!

Honoring

To Mary Wood

She had to take her nursing infant
with her to her final exam
because the babysitter hadn't shown up.

The professor threw her out,
but she completed her degree
and has been teaching for thirty years.

Now she is facing another exam,
one called cancer.

We, as mothers, daughters, and grandmothers,
are connected through our wombs.
We will stand with her, all of us together.
No one will throw her out.

Howling

Mysterious surprises us
when we least expect it:

the time when our husky
came to the kitchen.
Meat was smelling deliciously
throughout the room,
laughter was spicing up the walls,
and warmth spilled over our cups—

unlike his beginnings
in a cold, desert place
smelling of rock and dirt,
smelling of shivering and starvation.

But now you have come
in from the cold, haven't you?
And you are howling with your pack—
a mysterious howling that says,
all is right with the world.

Letter From the Earth

Today
I found a letter
from the earth.
It had my name
and address on it.

We must separate,
you and I, it said.
You no longer
stroke the side of my face
and watch for my coming.

You are lusting after another,
the one called Greed
and Selfishness.
I no longer can be with mankind.

I said, "But wait!
We must try again.
See,
I am mending my ways."

The earth
did not reply.

Life

We don't lead this life.
Life leads us
to places
where we don't know
how we'll end up.

We'll pack a light lunch
just in case.

Maple Sugar Moon

Maple sugar moon,
golden-eyed
like maple sap
boiling over wood fires,

finally,
you tell us
of the coming spring—
sweetness that brings
satisfaction,

one more year
to get things right.

Missing

The tenacious wren
slipped between
the red-fox's jaws,
dived between
the red squirrel's paws.

Before we turned around,
we missed her young
sitting on top of a shrub,
readying themselves
for their long journey ahead.

Just as we nod off,
we miss our chance
to prepare ourselves
for our long journey,
for the things that really matter in this world.

Never Again

Don't you remember?
Did you forget?
You said never again,
never again would we reduce
our brother and sister to rubble,
trash on the surface of the earth.

I'm sorry, but I think you've forgotten.
Now, we are that spider
hanging by a thread above the waters,
the waters of a rising river
filled with hate and rage,
and it is ready to devour us whole.

Path

Don't you know?
The earth will have
the final word.
She will read
the epitaph.

Quickly now.
There is little time left.

Look at that tree.
The earth has left sentinels
along the way
to keep us on the path.

Red Pine Bark

Red pine bark chips
fallen on frozen whiteness.

Nosey rabbit stops to stir them—
see if hawk comes out.

Retirement Party

To John Maggitti

He greeted everyone,
talking to them profusely,
looking directly into their eyes
and telling them exactly what he thought.
Telling us what we were worth.

We noticed a deep scar
running along his forehead
as we hugged him deeply.
He wanted all of us just
to put our arms around him.
So, we did.
We said our goodbyes.

A retirement party—not from work or a business,
but rather from the world of mankind.

Snowbound

All day it snowed.
At noon the children
ate their lunch in jars
heating on the wood stove
in the one-room schoolhouse.

At the end of the day, we were dismissed
and was pleased to see our father
with horses and a stoneboat,
glad we didn't have to walk
the mile-and-a-half home
back through the snow.

The stoneboat glided
through the snow like a sled.
We took many children home that day.

At home we bedded the horses down
with straw and plenty of hay to eat.
We were glad to be in a warm house
with a mother and father that cared enough
to bring us through the snowstorm.

The Speed of Light

When a hawk appears
in the corner
of their sky world,
songbirds calculate
how much time it takes
to find safe cover
in a split second
to find sanctuary.

Those in war-torn lands,
when they hear
screaming missiles
raining down,
don't have time to seek refuge,
not even at the speed of light.

Where My Heart Lies

Horse,
I will take you to a place
where there is an abundance of water,
where you can drink and eat
to your heart's content.

No, I cannot go there.
You cannot take hepatica
and place it in your sculptured garden,
for it will die
without the sunny woods and fallen trees.

I, too, will die
without the drum and dragon-fly dance,
away from my ancestors
in the high brittle desert.

I, too, will die,
for that is
where my heart lies.

You Would Be Happy, Francha

Poem written after Teresa Lind's sculpture, "Water Goddess Storm"

You would be happy, Francha,
for those gathered today
around the stormy sculptures.
A storm in a hatband you were.

All you wanted was justice,
didn't you?
A voice for those who
would not or could not stand up.

You would be happy, Francha
for the monarch butterflies
circling the art for you.
You, a lover of the earth
and all the creatures in it.

You would be happy
for those gathering today
to relish the essence of you
that lingers still.

Present

Has summer ended?
Have I missed autumn?

There is not a fine line drawn between seasons
but a bleeding of one into another,
a wave breaking and becoming another wave.

Yesterday, my heart was empty,
but today the chants from cranes high in the air
have filled my heart.

To be present, to hear them calling to each other
among the brightly colored maples—an artist's dream.

There is Still Time

But there is still a sunrise this morning,
red for rain.

We can still count the stars in Orion
and see the night sky.

There is still a dog at the end of the bed.
He is a guardian of our souls.

There is time to reach beyond smallness
that resides in our hearts.

ABOUT THE AUTHOR

    Ethel Mortenson Davis has had seven books of poetry published: *I Sleep Between the Moons of New Mexico*, *White Ermine Across Her Shoulders*, *Here We Breathe in Sky and Out Sky*, *The Healer*, *Under the Tail of the Milky Way Galaxy*, a 2019 Wisconsin Library Association outstanding book of poetry (all by Four Windows Press), and *A Letter on the Horizon's Poem* (Kelsay Books). Her last book, *A Gatherer*, included both poetry and full color reproductions of twelve of her abstract pastels. Her poems have also appeared in magazines, anthologies, and small literary journals.

    As an artist, she majored in art at the University of Wisconsin-Madison where she studied under the Twentieth Century abstract master Milton Resnick. Her work has appeared in small galleries, literary journals, and on the covers of several books by various authors.

    She was born in Wisconsin where her parents were dairy farmers in Marathon County. Her years on the farm instilled a deep sense of the earth, both wild and domestic animals, and different forms of life. Today she lives with her husband, Tom Davis, in Sturgeon Bay, Wisconsin.

    In 2010, her son, Kevin, passed away from cancer. She has two daughters, Sonja Bingen and Mary Wood, both teachers, and four grandchildren, Sophia Saucedo, and Phoebe Wood and Will and Joey Bingen. She also remains close to her three sisters, Beverly Mueller, Lorraine Wells, and Patricia Fennell.

www.ingramcontent.com/pod-product-compliance
Lightning Source LLC
Chambersburg PA
CBHW020603030426
42337CB00013B/1192